Beyond Boundaries
The Rushma Kafley Story

Rushma Kafley

Dedication

I would like to thank my mom and my whole family, who have been there for me in every situation, especially my mom!

Acknowledgment

I would like to express my deepest gratitude to everyone who has played a significant role in my journey. First and foremost, I thank my mother, whose unwavering love and determination have been the cornerstone of my life. Her strength in overcoming numerous challenges and her relentless fight for my rights and well-being have shaped me into the person I am today. Her resilience and love are beyond words, and I owe my successes to her sacrifices and support.

To my father, your courage and steadfastness in standing by our family despite the numerous obstacles have been a source of inspiration. Your decision to prioritize the well-being of our family, even in the face of difficult choices, is something I deeply admire and appreciate.

My sister, Isha, has been my protector and my friend. Her bravery during the fire and her constant support throughout my childhood have provided me with the strength to face the world. Her willingness to fight for me against bullies and her companionship have made my journey less lonely and more bearable.

I am also grateful to my best friends, Lokey and Sano, whose friendship and acceptance have shown me the true meaning of companionship. Their kindness and the way they treated me like any other person have left a lasting impact on my life. Lokey and Sano, you taught me the value of genuine friendship and acceptance, and for that, I am eternally thankful.

To Mrs. Tkach, your patience, kindness, and support during my transition to life in America were invaluable. You made me feel safe and understood, and your belief in my potential has encouraged me to aim high and pursue my dreams. Your reassuring words and support have been a guiding light in my educational journey.

Lastly, I want to thank all my teachers, friends, and everyone who has believed in me and supported me. Your encouragement has fueled my determination to succeed and to make a difference in the lives of others. I am committed to becoming a teacher for children with special needs and being an inspiration, just as my mother was to me. Thank you for being a part of my unique story.

About the Author

Rushma Kafley emerges as a beacon of hope and inspiration. Her journey from the heart of India to Nepal and to the United States symbolizes the triumph of the human spirit against all odds. Despite encountering myriad challenges along the way, Rushma's unwavering determination and unyielding faith in herself propel her forward, underscoring the profound resilience that resides within her. Integral to Rushma's narrative is the profound influence of her mother, whose unwavering support, sacrificial love, and untiring efforts influenced Rushma's life positively.

Preface

My name is Rushma Kafley, and I invite you on a journey through my life—a story of resilience, determination, and the unyielding power of love. Born in Assam, India, on March 9, 2004, my life began in humble and challenging circumstances. My mother, a remarkable woman of strength and courage, brought me into this world alone in our small kitchen. Her bravery in the face of adversity set the tone for the extraordinary path my life would take.

From the earliest days, my life was marked by trials. Diagnosed with cerebral palsy due to medicine my mother needed during her pregnancy, I faced physical challenges that set me apart from my peers. Despite the doctor's grim prognosis, my mother became my unwavering advocate and hero. She carried me on her back as she worked in the fields and devised innovative ways to help me gain strength and balance. Her relentless support and love were my foundation.

Our family's journey took us from India to Nepal, where we lived in a refugee camp. My father's Indian citizenship complicated our status, delaying our move to the United States. During these years, my parents shielded me from the harsh judgments of society, waking me before dawn for exercises to avoid the ridicule of others. Despite societal challenges, I found solace and inspiration in my family's love, particularly from my mother and my sister, Isha, who often protected me from bullies.

At the age of seven, I defied the odds and began to walk. This milestone opened doors for me, allowing me to attend regular school despite continued bullying and social obstacles. My sister, Isha, and my best friend, Sabina, stood by my side, offering friendship and support when I needed it most.

In 2016, my family and I finally arrived in America, where I faced new challenges but also found new allies, like Mrs. Tkach, who became my support person and a source of encouragement. As I navigated through middle and high school, her words and the love of my family fortified my spirit.

My story is one of overcoming adversity, inspired by my mother's resilience and the hope that I can make a difference. I aim to become a teacher for children with special needs, carrying forward the legacy of strength and compassion that my mother embodied. I am proud of who I am and embrace my journey with gratitude and hope for the future.

Contents

Chapter 1: A Unique Beginning

Growing up, I often heard the story of how my parents met, a tale that seems to weave through the fabric of our family's history, bringing smiles and nods of understanding whenever it's retold. Let me share it with you, just as it was passed down to me, filled with the simplicity and warmth of a love story that crossed paths and traditions.

At the ripe age of 24, my dad found himself on a journey across India, a quest not just of self-discovery but with the significant purpose of finding a wife. This wasn't merely about companionship; it was about finding someone who could shoulder the responsibilities of a burgeoning family, a person who could care for his home and the loved ones within it. My dad, you see, had been the man of the house from a very young age, his mother having passed away when he was just seven. Left with the responsibility of his younger siblings, he carried the weight of ensuring their well-being, especially his younger brother, whom he was determined to see educated and successful despite the absence of formal education in his own life.

In our culture, marriage is not just a union of two hearts but two families and, sometimes, even two communities. My dad's search was not just about finding a bride; it was about finding a partner who could blend into our family, bringing warmth and care to a home that had seen its share of hardships.

On the other side of this story, in a starkly different setting, was my mom. Picture a young girl of 17 living in a refugee camp in Nepal. Despite the humble surroundings, my mom stood out, not just for her beauty, which was the talk of the town, but for her resilience and spirit. She was in her 11th grade, a beacon of hope and strength for her family, her skin a shade lighter than most around her, making her beauty not just seen but talked about. Her grace and simplicity made her not just attractive but truly beautiful.

The twist in their tale came when my dad visited his cousin, who happened to be married to my mom's sister in Nepal. Yes, a small world, isn't it? There, amidst the simplicity of daily life, my dad set eyes on my mom for the first time. It wasn't love at first sight, at least not for my mom. With his robust physique and confident demeanor, my dad seemed to her like a player, a perception that initially made her wary of his advances.

But love, as they say, finds a way. My dad, determined as ever, was not put off by her initial rebuffs. Instead, he saw in her not just a pretty face but a soulmate who could share life's burdens and joys with him.

As the story unfolds, the delicate dance of courtship between my mom, Chandra, and my dad, Gyanu, is revealed. It takes on new complexities amidst the backdrop of family dynamics and societal expectations. Despite my mom's initial reluctance, my dad's persistent yet respectful advances painted a picture of budding affection, albeit one shrouded in misunderstanding and rumor.

The turning point in their tale came during a seemingly ordinary moment, an act as simple as sharing food at a family dinner. In our culture, such gestures, though small, can be laden with meaning, symbolizing care and a desire to provide. My dad's offer of untouched food to my mom was a tender act of kindness, yet it became the catalyst for rumors that would alter the course of their lives.

Whispers of an affair between Gyanu and Chandra began to circulate, fueled by the watchful eyes of family members eager to interpret every interaction as a sign of clandestine romance. The rumor mill, once started, was relentless. It reached a crescendo when my aunt, misled by tales spun by her sister-in-law, misconstrued their relationship and confronted my mom with a slap—a harsh response to a misunderstood situation.

The irony of the situation was palpable. My dad's attempts at kindness, meant to bridge the gap between them, instead sparked a series of events that highlighted the fragility of reputation and the swift judgments of those around them. Faced with the fallout, my dad proposed again, framing their predicament as an unintended consequence of their affection for one another. He suggested marriage as a solution, a bold step that would both shield them from further gossip and solidify their bond.

Driven by a mix of defiance and a newfound realization of their feelings, they made a decision that was as daring as it was decisive—they ran away together. This act of elopement was a testament to their willingness to defy norms and stand against the tide of family disapproval for the sake of their love. They sought refuge with my dad's sister in Nepal, choosing a path that would lead them away from the familiar and into the unknown.

Their journey to Nepal signified more than a mere physical relocation; it represented a symbolic leap into a future they would shape together, free from the constraints of their past lives.

The repercussions of their elopement reverberated through their families, leaving a trail of anger and concern for reputations tarnished by their unorthodox union. Yet, amidst the turmoil, my parents' resolve remained unshaken. They understood the weight of their decision, recognizing that the path to happiness is often fraught with obstacles but believing in the strength of their bond to overcome them.

After eloping, my parents found refuge in the warmth of my dad's family, particularly with his third sister. Despite the initial shock and her stern reprimand toward my dad for the audacious act of eloping, she soon became a pillar of support, especially for my mom. In a world that seemed against them, my aunt stood out as a beacon of kindness and understanding. She extended a hand of friendship and solidarity to my mom, offering her clothes and a sense of belonging in those early days of uncertainty.

Their journey then took them to New Delhi, the bustling capital of India, where the magic of the city seemed to weave its own spell around their relationship. It was here, amidst the ancient temples and the vibrant chaos of the city, that they truly fell in love with each other. Their love, which had begun as a series of tentative steps overshadowed by societal norms and expectations, now flourished in the open, unfettered by the judgments of others. They sealed their bond in a sacred ceremony at a Hindu temple, a testament to their commitment and the start of a shared life path.

Life in New Delhi was a period of growth and deepening bonds, a time for my parents to explore the depths of their love and build their family's foundations. But the call of home, of returning to Assam to introduce my mom to the rest of the family, was strong. After a year, they journeyed back to my dad's ancestral home, where the reception was warmer and more welcoming than they could have hoped. My mom, once viewed with suspicion and doubt, was now embraced as a cherished member of the family. My grandfather, in particular, treated her with a tenderness and affection that belied the initial turmoil surrounding their union. He saw in her not just the wife of his son but a daughter in her own right, a beloved addition to the family.

The joy of their acceptance in Assam was soon amplified by the arrival of my sister, a symbol of the love between my parents and a bridge between their past struggles and their hopes for the future. My sister's birth, when my mom was just 17, marked the beginning of a new chapter in their lives, one filled with the responsibilities and joys of parenthood.

After three years, in the quietude of an ordinary day, my life began in a way that was anything but ordinary. Nestled in the heart of Assam, India, amidst the verdant landscape that stretched as far as the eye could see, my first breath was drawn in the humble confines of our family kitchen. It was here, surrounded by the simple trappings of rural life, that my story took root.

My mother, a young woman of just twenty, found herself alone on that pivotal day, the 9th of March, 2004. With my sister away and my father tending to the day's demands, she was our family's solitary anchor. Earlier that morning, she had been engaged in the day's routine, moving with the rhythm of rural life, from milking the cows to attending to the hearth. Yet, as the day unfolded, she found herself facing the monumental task of bringing a new life into the world, with nothing but her own resolve to guide her.

It was a night wrapped in the ordinary, under a sky jeweled with stars, when the extraordinary decided to make its entrance. My story began at around nine, maybe half past, under the humble roof of our wooden and mud kitchen, where the ordinary act of preparing a meal was about to intertwine with the miraculous act of giving life.

My mother, alone in the warmth of our rustic kitchen, was tending to the evening's meal. The simplicity of our home, constructed from the earth itself—wood and mud—echoed the simplicity of our lives. We were rich in land, with fields stretching out like a green sea, but our pockets were as empty as the night sky is of daylight. Our wealth was in the soil, the crops, and the livestock that roamed our farm, but money, the kind that fills hospitals and buys comfort, was a stranger to our dwelling.

That night, as the coolness of dusk settled over our land, my mother felt the first stirrings of my arrival. There was no stove, no modern convenience to aid her in her cooking; only a fire oven, a humble construction of dirt and necessity, where she prepared our meals with the hands that were soon to welcome me into the world.

The kitchen was modest, a sanctuary of both sustenance and now birth. The walls, made of wood and plastered with mud, stood a testament to our connection with the earth. It was here, in this simple setting, that the lines between strength and vulnerability, between everyday life and the extraordinary, blurred.

As the moments passed, the quiet of the night was broken by the symphony of our farm. Outside, the crickets sang their endless song, a melody punctuated by the croaks of frogs from the nearby pond. Perhaps sensing the shift in the air, the cows added their low moos to the nocturnal chorus, a comforting sound that spoke of home and familiarity. Even the chickens, usually silent in the embrace of night, seemed to sense the urgency of the moment, their clucks and rustles adding to the crescendo of life happening in real-time.

And then, there was my mother. Amid this symphony of the night, her strength became the melody. Alone, she faced the arrival of her child with a bravery that was as natural to her as breathing. Her screams, louder and more primal than any sound our farm had ever known, were not just expressions of pain but of fierce determination and unyielding courage.

The world outside, with its bugs and frogs, cows and chickens, seemed to pause, holding its breath as I made my entrance into it. My birth, unassisted and in the humblest of settings, was a testament to the resilience of the human spirit, the strength of a mother's love, and the beauty of life that flourishes even in the most modest circumstances.

The labor was a testament to her strength, a silent battle she faced without a witness, save for the walls of our modest kitchen. In those moments, fraught with the intensity of life's beginnings, she exemplified a resilience that would come to define the spirit of our family. With hands that had nurtured and toiled, she welcomed me into the world, severing the cord that bound us and embarking on a journey that was ours alone.

In the days that followed, no doctor would affirm my health, and no medical professional would marvel at the miracle of life. Our remoteness from the conveniences of modern medicine meant that my first cries were met not with clinical observation but with the intimate care of a mother's love. This was a time when the rhythms of nature dictated the ebb and flow of daily life, and my early days were cradled in this simplicity.

In life, each thread is woven with its own unique hues, creating patterns that speak to the journeys of those it represents. My thread, imbued with a blend of challenge and resilience, began to reveal its distinct pattern early in my life. It was a year after my silent entry into the world, amidst the verdant expanse of Assam, that my family started to notice the whispers of difference that set my path apart.

As a toddler, my world was one of constant discomfort, marked by cries that echoed through the modest confines of our home. With eyes honed by the intuition that comes from deep maternal bonds, my mother sensed that my journey was diverging from the expected milestones. The laughter and play of my cousin and neighbor, who were of the same age, starkly contrasted with my own struggles. Where they moved with the effortless grace of budding life, I remained ensconced in a silent battle, my cries a testament to the unseen hurdles I faced.

Growing up, life presented a series of relentless challenges, not just for me but profoundly more for my mother. This story, my story, is as much hers as it is mine, painting a vivid picture of resilience, love, and unwavering determination in the face of adversity.

My earliest memories are clouded with struggles, most notably my inability to crawl. This physical limitation, a precursor to my later diagnosis of cerebral palsy, meant that my world was confined to the small expanse of our humble home. My mother, a figure of slender build but immense strength, took it upon herself to ensure that my disability did not confine my experiences. She carried me on her back, a testament to her physical and emotional strength, as she navigated the daily challenges of our lives.

Our home was a bustling hub of never-ending tasks, with my mother at the helm. She was a whirlwind of activity, managing household chores with a kind of grace and efficiency that was nothing short of miraculous. Cooking, cleaning, and laundry were just the tip of the iceberg. We didn't have the luxury of modern appliances; every task was done by hand, with care and attention. Clothes were washed in basins, scrubbed, and rinsed until they were as clean as our modest means would allow.

But my mother's duties stretched far beyond the confines of our home. Our family owned a small piece of farming land, a precious asset that demanded hard work and dedication. Despite our ownership, our financial situation was dire. Poverty was a constant shadow over our lives, compelling my mother to seek additional work on neighboring farms. She balanced these demanding tasks with the precision of a tightrope walker, all while carrying the additional weight of my needs on her shoulders.

Farming was not just about tilling the land; it was about nurturing every aspect of our property to ensure our survival. My mother tended to the cows, chickens, and goats, her days starting before dawn and ending well after dusk. Milking cows, feeding the livestock, and managing the crops, she did it all with a relentless drive and a smile that seldom faded despite the exhaustion.

From birth, I was different. Jaundice marked my entry into the world, painting my skin a pale hue and signaling the start of our long journey with health challenges. Without the means to afford hospital care, my mother became my nurse and my guardian. She battled my health issues, facing each day with a resilience that was awe-inspiring. My constant crying, a byproduct of my discomfort and later understood to be linked to my cerebral palsy, was a soundtrack to our lives, yet she never wavered in her care or love.

Our family dynamic was complex. My father, consumed by his efforts to provide through his business, was often absent, leaving my mother to shoulder the responsibilities of our home. Additionally, she devoted her care to my older sister, Isha, who was already three years old when I was born, making me the youngest in the family. This arrangement further demanded her time and energy. Despite these challenges, she exhibited an almost superhuman capability, ensuring that both Isha and I felt loved, cared for, and valued without any siblings beyond us.

Reflecting on those years, it's clear that my mother's strength was the cornerstone of our family. Her ability to manage the household, contribute to our farming needs, and care for my sister and me, all while dealing with my health challenges, is nothing short of extraordinary. Her resilience, love, and dedication shaped my childhood and laid the foundation for the person I am today.

Growing up in a world that often felt too big and complex, I learned early on that my journey would be unlike others. My story isn't just about the challenges I faced but also about love, resilience, and the beauty of acceptance. Let me take you through my journey, a tale woven with the threads of struggle, discovery, and unconditional love.

My earliest memories are fragments, snapshots of moments filled with confusion and concern from the adults around me. I was like any other child in their eyes until milestones started to pass by, unnoticed by my little hands and feet. While other toddlers began exploring the world on all fours, crawling with eager curiosity, I remained stationary, an observer rather than a participant.

This phase of stillness wasn't just about mobility; it extended to my silence. Words, those magical sounds that seemed to flow effortlessly from others, eluded me. My family watched, their hearts tangled in worry as my first birthday came and went, with no words or steps to mark the occasion. It was a silence that spoke louder than words, echoing questions and fears about my future.

My mother, a pillar of strength and love, harbored the growing realization that my path was veering away from the so-called norm. Her intuition, honed by years of caring not just for me but for others in our community, whispered that my challenges were more than just late blooming. Her heart ached with the question of why her child remained locked in a world without speech or movement, a riddle she desperately sought to solve.

The answer came shrouded in a term that was both a diagnosis and a label: cerebral palsy. It was a revelation that shattered the silence with a thunderous impact, leaving my parents grappling with a reality they never anticipated. Their dreams for me were suddenly painted with strokes of uncertainty and fear, emotions that welled up and overflowed in silent prayers and tears.

The diagnosis was a storm that broke with little warning, leaving my family to navigate the unfamiliar waters of cerebral palsy. The doctor's words fell like rain, heavy with the sorrow of unexpected news. My condition, he explained, was likely the result of medication my mother had taken during her pregnancy, a bitter potion administered to save her life, yet harboring the potential to alter mine. Faced with the harrowing choice of losing his wife or risking the health of his unborn child, my father had chosen the path of love, a decision that now bore the weight of unintended consequences.

Despite the storm of emotions that this diagnosis stirred, my mother's love remained a beacon of unwavering light. She, who had dreamt of my first words and steps, found her strength not diminished but fortified. Her faith, deeply rooted in our Hindu beliefs, faced the ultimate test as she questioned the gods she devotedly worshipped. Yet, even in her anger and despair, she never ceased to pray for me, to hope for a miracle that might ease my journey.

My father, too, was a fortress of support and acceptance. The news that broke him also rebuilt him, molding him into the advocate and protector I needed. His words, "God made you unique," became our family's mantra, a declaration of acceptance and love that knew no bounds.

Among the many blessings in my life, my sister's presence shines the brightest. Born three years before me, she became not just a sibling but my best friend, my guardian, and my greatest ally. Even as a child, her understanding and empathy surpassed her years, providing me with a tender and empowering companionship.

Together, we navigated the complexities of the world, her youthful innocence and bravery facing down the shadows of my limitations. She was my voice when words failed me, my legs when the path seemed too daunting, and my laughter in moments of despair. In her, I found not just a sister but a soulmate, a constant reminder that family transcends the confines of ability.

As years passed, the initial shock of my diagnosis faded into a quiet acceptance woven into the fabric of our daily lives. Once shattered by the thought of my challenges, my parents found strength in their love for me and the resilience I displayed. Their journey from despair to acceptance mirrored my own, a path marked by small victories and immense challenges.

Their support, coupled with my sister's unwavering presence, taught me that my disability did not define me. I learned to see myself through their eyes—not as a child burdened by cerebral palsy, but as a unique individual capable of love, laughter, and dreams.

The revelation was a crucible, testing the strength and resilience of our family's bonds. My parents, faced with the reality of my condition, grappled with a maelstrom of emotions. Guilt, sorrow, and fear mingled with the unwavering love they held for me, each feeling a thread in the complex weave of our family's response.

The day the diagnosis was confirmed remains etched in memory, not for the words spoken by the doctor but for the palpable shift in the atmosphere. My parents, who had always been pillars of strength and joy, suddenly seemed to bear the weight of the world. Their faces, usually the source of comfort and warmth, were clouded with concern and uncertainty. Yet, beneath the veneer of worry, there was an unspoken vow, a promise that resonated with the depth of their love and the strength of their character.

This narrative, my beginning, is more than a tale of birth; it is a reflection of the unspoken bonds that tie us, the silent strength that propels us through life's challenges. It is a reminder that sometimes, the most profound stories are those that unfold in the quiet spaces of our lives, away from the gaze of the world.

As I share these words, I invite you to see beyond the simplicity of a birth story. Look into the heart of a young woman who, in her solitude, embraced the magnitude of life's most sacred act. See the resilience of a family, my family, whose beginnings were marked not by the ease of modern convenience but by the raw, unfiltered essence of human strength.

My journey began in silence, but it is a silence that speaks volumes. It is a testament to the indomitable spirit of those who came before me, a legacy of strength and resilience that I carry forward. As you walk through the chapters of my life, remember this beginning, for it is the foundation upon which my story is built.

Chapter 2: Early Challenges

Every step I couldn't take, my mother carried me through each one, teaching me that the strength of the human spirit is boundless, even when the body has its limits.

Growing up in a small village nestled between rolling hills and vast fields, my life was a testament to human resilience and the undying spirit of love that my mother embodied. She was not just my caretaker; she was my hero, my bridge over troubled waters, and the very essence of my strength. My disability, a constant companion from birth, meant that my legs could not carry me where my heart longed to go. Yet, it was through this journey, marked by challenges and misunderstandings, that I discovered the depth of societal stigma surrounding disabilities and, more importantly, the boundless love that can overcome it.

Each day dawned with the same routine, but no day was ever truly the same. My mother, a figure of unwavering strength, would carry me on her back as she ventured into the fields to work. There, amidst the golden waves of grain and under the watchful gaze of the sun, she toiled with me securely strapped to her, never once complaining, never once faltering. In those moments, feeling the warmth of her back and the steady rhythm of her steps, I felt most connected to her and to the earth that sustained us.

In our village, where everyone knew everyone else's business, our situation was a topic of continuous discussion and, often, of pity. I could see it in their eyes, the way they looked at me and then at my mother, with a mix of sympathy and something else—

perhaps discomfort or even disdain. It was a silent acknowledgment of the societal stigma attached to my disability, an unspoken agreement that I was different in a way that was not acceptable to them.

This stigma was not confined to mere glances or whispered conversations behind closed backs. It manifested in more tangible, sometimes hurtful ways. Unfiltered and uninhibited children would often ask why I couldn't run and play with them, their innocence not masking the sting of their words. Adults, on the other hand, offered unsolicited advice to my mother, suggesting treatments, prayers, and sometimes, even miracles, as if my condition was a problem to be solved rather than a part of who I am.

But my mother taught me the most valuable lesson of all— that love transcends the physical realm. She crafted a world for me where my disability did not define me. In her wisdom, she dug a hole in the ground, deep enough and narrow enough, so that I could stand up and keep my balance. This simple act, born out of necessity and ingenuity, was my first step toward independence. Standing there, in that hole, I felt a semblance of what it might be like to stand on my own, to not be defined by my limitations but by the possibilities that lay within me.

As I grew older, I began to understand the depth of the societal stigma we faced. It was a multifaceted beast woven into the fabric of our community through ignorance, misunderstanding, and fear. People feared what they did not understand, and they did not understand disability. To them, it was a curse, a burden that one had to bear for the person directly affected and their family. They failed to see the person behind the disability, the dreams, aspirations, and desires that were no different from their own.

This misunderstanding impacted my daily life in profound ways. It was not just the physical barriers that held me back but the societal ones as well. Opportunities for education or for social interaction were limited, not by my capabilities, but by the perceptions of those around me. It was a constant battle, not just for physical survival, but for recognition, for the right to be seen as a full and equal member of society.

From the moment I was born, my mother knew I was special. Not in the way that all parents think their child is special, but in a deep, visceral sense that something about my life would be extraordinary. She told me about a time when she was at her wit's end, trying to understand the path her life and mine were meant to take. That's when she decided to visit a fortune teller, seeking clarity or perhaps a glimpse into what the future held for me, her youngest child, Rushma.

The day was etched in her memory, clear as the bright sky on that warm afternoon. She always described it with a mix of apprehension and hope. Carrying me in her arms, she stepped into the dimly lit room, the air thick with the scent of incense and a palpable tension that made her heart race. The fortune teller, an elderly man with insightful eyes, didn't take long after seeing us to make his prophecy known.

"If Rushma walks by the age of seven," he had said, "she will do something in life that people will be proud of, and everyone will know her by name. If she does not walk by seven years, she will be a big problem for you and your family."

Heavy with implication, those words settled in my mother's heart like a stone. She left the fortune teller's place with me still in her arms, silent and contemplative. It was a moment that would define our lives in ways neither of us could have imagined.

At first, she didn't tell anyone about the prophecy. It was her secret, a burden she chose to carry alone. But as I grew older and struggled to meet the milestones expected of a child my age, the weight of the fortune teller's words grew heavier. Watching me, she was torn between despair and hope. Despair because with each passing day, my inability to walk seemed to seal my fate as a "problem" for our family. Hope, because she refused to let a prophecy dictate our lives.

Determined to prove destiny wrong, my mother became my beacon of hope and determination. She dedicated herself to supporting my journey against all odds.

Her resolve was contagious. Even as a child, I could feel the strength of her conviction, and it spurred me on. I wanted to walk, not just for myself, but for her. To prove that the fortune teller's prophecy would not define my life or my worth. My mother's unwavering support became the foundation upon which I built my determination.

In the years that followed, my mother often reflected on that day with the fortune teller. Though daunting, she believed that his words had ignited a fire within her, a determination to fight for my future regardless of the outcome. It wasn't about proving him right or wrong; it was about refusing to accept a predetermined fate for her child.

That prophecy, which could have been a source of despair, became our rallying cry. It taught us the power of hope and the strength of a mother's love. It showed us that the future is not written in stone but is something we have the power to shape through our actions and beliefs.

Today, as I look back on those challenging early years, I see them not as a time of struggle but as a period of growth and immense love. My mother's belief in me, her refusal to let me be defined by a prophecy, has shaped the person I am. Her support has been my constant, her strength my guide. Together, we've proved that we can overcome even the most daunting predictions with love, determination, and a bit of defiance.

The fortune teller's prophecy did indeed come true, but not in the way he or anyone else expected. I have achieved things in my life that have made my mother proud, and yes, many people know my name. But more importantly, they know our story—a story of hope, determination, and the unbreakable bond between a mother and her child. It's a story I now share, not as a tale of destiny or fate but as a testament to the power of belief and its incredible impact on our lives.

My condition, a constant companion, set me apart from my peers in ways that went beyond what meets the eye. Yet, despite the hurdles, my family embarked on a relentless mission to weave a fabric of normalcy and inclusion around my life, challenging both my condition and the societal prejudices that often came with it. This is a glimpse into that journey—a simple, straightforward account of resilience, love, and the pursuit of normalcy.

From the earliest days I can remember, my family turned our home into a sanctuary. It was a place where my condition did not define me; instead, it was just another characteristic, like having black hair or brown eyes. My parents, siblings, and extended family members all played their roles in this carefully orchestrated endeavor. They were the architects of a world where I was not just included but celebrated for who I was, my condition, and all.

But it was within these struggles that I learned resilience. I saw firsthand the power of advocacy and the importance of standing up for one's rights. My family's efforts taught me that while the world might not always be welcoming, there are always pathways to inclusion if one is willing to fight for them.

Outside of home, my family navigated the broader societal prejudices with a mix of defiance and grace. We encountered stares, whispers, and outright discrimination in public spaces. Yet, my parents used these moments as teachable opportunities, not just for me but for those around us. They would engage in conversations with strangers, challenging their prejudices and advocating for a more inclusive society.

These experiences were not without their emotional toll. There were days when the weight of my differences felt crushing, when the stares and whispers seemed too much to bear. In those days, my family's support was unwavering. They were there to listen, to comfort, and to remind me of my worth beyond my condition. In these moments of vulnerability, the true depth of their efforts shone through.

As I grew older, the emphasis shifted from merely ensuring inclusion to empowering me to advocate for myself. My family supported me in exploring my interests, encouraging me to pursue hobbies and activities that resonated with me. They stood by me as I navigated the complexities of friendships and relationships, offering guidance but also the freedom to learn from my own experiences.

Looking back, the journey of my family to provide me with a semblance of normalcy and inclusion amidst the challenges posed by my condition and societal prejudices is a testament to the power of love and determination. It was not about denying the realities of my condition but rather about refusing to let it limit the breadth of my experiences.

In sharing this story, my aim is not to portray my family as heroes but rather to highlight the everyday acts of inclusion and normalcy that can make a significant difference in someone's life. It's a call to action for society to embrace diversity, not as a challenge to be overcome but as an opportunity to enrich our collective human experience.

This journey of inclusion and normalcy is ongoing, and the challenges have evolved as I've grown. Yet, my family's foundation has given me the strength and resilience to face them head-on. It's a reminder that while the world may not always be kind or understanding, there are always pockets of love and acceptance to be found. And sometimes, those pockets are closer than we think, nestled within the walls of our own homes.

Chapter 3: A New Homeland

When I was just four years old, my world was small, yet it felt immense, filled with wonders, fears, love, and challenges. At that tender age, I lived in India, a place vibrant with colors and life, where every day was a lesson in survival and familial bonds. My mother was my universe, nurturing and caring, while my grandfather was a pillar of strength and wisdom, assisting my mother in my upbringing.

The earliest memory that etches itself vividly in my mind is of a night that seemed like any other, but for me, it was filled with an adventure and a fear so intense that it left an indelible mark on me. It was the night my mother went out to milk the cow, a routine task in our rural life, yet something extraordinary happened. She placed me on the kitchen floor, close to the warmth of the fire that flickered and danced, casting shadows that played on the walls. I sat there, mesmerized by the flames, unaware of the small drama about to unfold.

My tranquility was shattered when a frog, perhaps lured by the light or in search of its own adventure, decided to leap toward me. To a four-year-old, that frog was a creature of nightmares; its sudden appearance and the prospect of its cold, slimy touch sent me into a state of panic. In my desperate attempt to escape, I nearly stumbled into the fire. It was my mother's quick intervention that saved me from harm, her arms pulling me back into the safety of her embrace. That night, the lessons were clear: the world was full of surprises, some pleasant, others terrifying, and the comfort of a mother's arms was the safest haven.

Life continued in its complex, unpredictable rhythm. My days were filled with small tasks, lessons from my mother, and stories from my grandfather. But the fabric of our family changed irrevocably when my grandfather passed away. I was only four, yet the weight of his absence bore down on us. He had been a source of joy, wisdom, and support. With him gone, the void was palpable, and the challenges we faced seemed to magnify.

It was around this time that the wider family dynamics began to shift. My mother, resilient and determined, received a call from her family in Nepal. It was a call that bridged distances and brought to light the realities we faced, including my own challenges and the disability program that might offer me support. The conversation opened the door to a new beginning, a chance for us to be part of a larger community and find support and understanding in the embrace of extended family.

The decision was made to move to Nepal to join my mother's family in a refugee camp. This decision was not made lightly. The journey itself was an adventure, a day-long train ride that promised a reunion with family members I had never met, including my maternal grandparents. The prospect of meeting them filled me with a mixture of excitement and apprehension. What would life be like in Nepal? How would we adjust to living in a refugee camp?

The camp was a world unto itself, a place of contrasts where life was neither good nor bad but somewhere in between. It was here, in this new, unfamiliar environment, that I met my maternal grandparents for the first time. Their presence brought a sense of continuity, linking the past with the present and offering a glimpse into a future filled with potential.

It was the year I turned five when my family faced the daunting decision that would alter the course of our lives forever. We were living in India, a country of vast diversity and rich cultural heritage. Yet, the promise of a brighter future beckoned us from afar, compelling us to embark on a journey fraught with uncertainty and hope.

The decision wasn't made on a whim. Discussions filled with anxious voices and hopeful whispers painted the walls of our modest home. My parents, particularly my mother, wrestled with the heart-wrenching dilemma of leaving everything familiar behind. The prospect of moving to a Nepali refugee camp as a stepping stone to the United States held a gleam of opportunity, an allure too potent to dismiss.

My grandparents, on my mother's side, urged us to join them, painting a picture of a collective effort to raise the children and the tantalizing possibility of one day making it to America. This dream, distant yet alluring, became a beacon of hope for my parents, a promise of opportunities and a life far removed from the struggles we faced daily.

Upon arrival in the refugee camp, the reality of our new life began to unfold. The camp, with its closely packed houses made of bamboo and roofs of plastic, was a stark contrast to our previous home. The simplicity of the structures belied the complexity of life within. Rainfall brought leaks, turning our living space into a testament to resilience as we navigated the challenges of daily existence in such an environment.

My uncle, a figure of kindness and support, joined us in this new chapter. My father made significant sacrifices, giving up property and the familiarity of home for the sake of our future. It was a testament to his love and dedication to our family, a sacrifice for the promise of a better life ahead, not just in Nepal but with sights set on America.

In the camp, curiosity and sometimes judgment from our neighbors became a part of our daily lives. People wondered about my condition, their inquiries often laced with a lack of understanding. My mother, protective and wise, devised strategies to shield me from such scrutiny. She woke me early when the camp was still enveloped in the quiet of dawn to practice walking. This routine, set before the world awoke, was her way of protecting me from prying eyes and unnecessary questions, a buffer against the judgment we feared.

My middle uncle emerged as a beacon of support during these times. Not only did he assist with my physical challenges, creating a path for me to walk and gain balance, but he also took on a nurturing role, especially when my mother sought employment to support us. His efforts, combined with my mother's unwavering dedication, painted a picture of familial love and sacrifice that defined my early years.

Education became a focal point in our struggle for a better future. Without access to specialized transportation, my mother carried me on her back to school, enduring the heat and the weight, driven by a singular goal: to ensure I received the education and therapy I needed. This journey, taken under the harsh sun, was a testament to her dedication, a daily ritual that spoke volumes of her love and determination for me to thrive against all odds.

Fast forward to 2008, my mother's family had migrated to America, leaving us as the remnants of a once-united family tree on Nepali soil. My father, born in Bhutan and raised in India, faced an insurmountable barrier. His identity as a non-refugee meant he was ineligible for the refugee status that could pave our way to the United States.

Authorities presented a solution as cold as it was clear: my mother could emigrate with her daughters if she divorced my father. Such a proposition was unthinkable, an affront to the very essence of what our family stood for. "This is not an option," my mother declared, her voice a blend of defiance and determination. We would not be fractured by borders or bureaucracies.

The ensuing years were a testament to my mother's relentless spirit. She embarked on a formidable journey to secure my father's rights to ensure we could step onto American soil as a unified family. This quest, however, anchored us to Nepal for an extended period, far longer than we had anticipated.

My mother played many roles in my life: nurse, teacher, protector, and advocate. Her actions, often unseen by the wider world, laid the foundation for my development and learning. She introduced me to sign language, supported my special education needs, and became the bridge to the world I needed to navigate.

As I began to find my voice, a new challenge presented itself: my words were a mystery to everyone except my mother. She became my translator, my mediator to the outside world, understanding me when no one else could. This unique and unbreakable bond was my lifeline, allowing me to express myself through her interpretation. Despite the communication barrier with others, we persisted, fueled by an unwavering resolve to connect and be understood.

During this period of personal growth and adaptation, my mother's side of the family succeeded in their journey to the United States, leaving us behind due to my father's different origins. He was not from the refugee camp, complicating our eligibility for resettlement. My mother, ever the fighter, championed our cause, arguing that our family unit should not be disqualified from seeking a new life in America. This battle, however, slowed our progress, adding another layer of complexity to our already challenging situation.

Amidst these struggles, disaster struck in the form of a devastating fire within our community. A simple act of faith — a lady lighting a candle in prayer — turned catastrophic when the candle was accidentally knocked over, igniting a blaze that consumed our town. The fire forced us to flee, seeking safety and shelter far from the ashes of what was once our home. We eventually found a new house, a place to restart and rebuild our lives amidst the chaos.

In this new home, the physical challenges of my condition became more pronounced. My attempts to walk were fraught with falls, leading to numerous injuries. Yet, with each fall, my determination only grew stronger. I refused to be defined by my limitations, pushing myself to stand and try again despite the pain and frustration. My speech, still misunderstood by many, became a source of anger for me. However, my mother, ever patient and understanding, would gently explain my words to others, bridging the gap between my thoughts and the world.

Driven by a desire to support me fully, my mother embarked on a remarkable journey of her own. She sought out training in special education and occupational therapy, traveling far and wide to gather knowledge and skills. She brought these lessons home, applying them to our daily routine, teaching me how to walk, talk, and engage with the world around me. Her dedication knew no bounds; she was my teacher, my therapist, and my unwavering supporter.

Through it all, my love for her grew immeasurably. She was my beacon in the darkest times, guiding me through the challenges with a grace and strength that I admired deeply. Her sacrifices, her unwavering belief in me, and her tireless efforts to improve our lives were a testament to the depth of her love and dedication. As we faced each obstacle, our bond deepened, rooted in mutual respect, love, and an unbreakable resolve to overcome the odds together. My mother was not just my caregiver; she was my hero, the person who taught me that love, in its purest form, knows no limits.

By the age of seven or eight, with encouragement from my indefatigable mother, I had started to walk. My steps were unsteady, marked by frequent falls due to my balance issues. Yet, it was through laughter—a buoyant, infectious laughter—that I found the strength to persevere. My older sister, who was three years my senior, became another source of joy and inspiration in my life. She absorbed in the discipline of dance and would return home from her classes eager to share the steps she had learned, transforming our living room into a stage of exploration and mimicry.

Observing my sister's dances, my mother saw no reason why I shouldn't participate in such joys. Driven by her unwavering belief in equality and her conviction that I deserved every chance to pursue my interests, she approached my sister's dance teacher, advocating for my inclusion. Despite my initial excitement, the dance class proved to be a realm of challenge beyond the physical. The teacher, lacking understanding and patience, quickly voiced doubts about my ability to participate, his words cutting deeper than any physical stumble could.

Returning home in tears after being subjected to the teacher's insensitive remarks, I questioned my mother, seeking solace in her wisdom. "Why can't people just look at me the way they look at other people?" I asked, feeling the weight of being perceived as different. Her response was a beacon in the storm, affirming my uniqueness as a divine gift, a special talent that set me apart in a fabulous way. Bolstered by her words, my mother confronted the teacher the following day, defending my dignity and right to dance. Yet, despite her advocacy, I was hesitant to return to a place where I felt so misunderstood.

Around this time, my sister's nurturing spirit shone brightly. Despite being only nine, she took it upon herself to include me in the cultural life of our community. She would learn about local dance and cultural programs, carrying me on her back to these events, ensuring I could experience the joy of music and movement alongside her. This act of sisterly love was more than just a means of transportation; it was an affirmation of my right to joy, participation, and belonging.

My sister has always been more than just a sibling to me; she's my first best friend, a beacon of strength and compassion in a world that often seemed too harsh. Our bond was tested and solidified through trials that many could scarcely imagine, one of which was another devastating fire that swept through our refugee camp.

I remember vividly when disaster struck for the second time. My father was away, and my mother was occupied with her noble work, leaving my sister and me to face the emergency alone. We were at school when the flames began to consume our town again, a terrifying déjà vu that no child should ever have to experience. At ten years old, my sister once again became my protector, carrying me on her back, not just away from the flames but toward safety and comfort. Her actions in those moments were a testament to her incredible courage and love.

In an attempt to escape the encroaching fire, she took me to a forest near a mountain, a place she deemed safe enough for us to wait. There, amidst the uncertainty and fear, my mother found us, her relief palpable as she embraced us, grateful for our safety. This moment, though fraught with fear, showcased the indomitable spirit of my family and our will to survive and protect each other against all odds.

The aftermath of the fire left us with nothing. Our house, like many others, was reduced to ashes, leaving us without shelter, food, or clean clothes. The community was enveloped in smoke, a grim reminder of the disaster that had just occurred. In the days that followed, we sought refuge in the forest, a temporary shelter from the chaos that had engulfed our lives. This period of displacement, while challenging, was also a time of profound bonding and resilience as we faced the stark reality of our situation together.

With our home gone, we had to start anew. We constructed a makeshift shelter out of plastic, a humble abode that served as a temporary refuge as we planned our next steps. Our journey then took us to another refugee camp, prompted by an invitation from my father's cousin, who offered us food and shelter. This move marked the beginning of another chapter in our lives, a fresh start in a new camp that promised a semblance of stability and hope.

In this new refugee camp, my story continued to unfold, filled with lessons of strength, hope, and the enduring power of love and resilience. As we navigated this new chapter, I was reminded of the importance of holding onto hope, of believing in the possibility of a brighter future, and of the incredible strength that comes from family and the will to survive.

Chapter 4: Battles and Belonging

My journey to education was not a path paved with ease but one filled with obstacles that seemed insurmountable at times. Raised in a refugee camp, my early years were encapsulated within bamboo walls that whispered stories of resilience and survival. This camp was my universe, a place teeming with life and the echoes of shared destinies. Extended by the bonds of community and circumstance, my family found solace in each other's presence. Among these familiar faces were my father's cousin. Their presence a constant reminder of faith and hope amidst uncertainty.

There were two lychee trees outside our house. Adjacent to our home stood a birdhouse, once a bustling pigeon house, that faced our front door. It was a simple structure, yet it held the echoes of days when people gathered, spinning stories as they operated the yarn winder machine, intertwining threads as they shaped their lives. Although not my initial steps, at the age of nine, I began to walk unaided, without the security of holding hands. Despite my unsteady balance, each step was a profound stride toward the autonomy I longed for—pursuing an education.

My mother, a pillar of strength and unwavering support, decided it was time for me to start school. Despite my physical limitations, she saw in me a spark of potential that she was determined to nurture. With hope in her heart and me by her side, we made our way to the school within the camp to enroll me in first grade at Marigold Academy School. The anticipation of what lay ahead filled me with a mixture of excitement and apprehension.

However, our hopes were met with resistance. The principal, citing concerns over my physical capabilities, suggested that a special needs school would be more suited to my situation. The notion that I would be denied access to the same education as my peers solely because of my physical condition was disheartening. But my mother, undeterred, stood her ground. She looked the principal in the eyes and spoke with a conviction that resonated with every fiber of her being. "My daughter may have physical challenges, but her mind is sharp, and her spirit is unbreakable. She is smart, she is capable, and she deserves the same opportunity to learn as any other child here," she asserted with unwavering confidence.

Her words, spoken with such fierce determination, struck a chord. She promised to be by my side, to assist me with my needs, and to ensure that my education would not be hindered by my physical limitations. Her advocacy on my behalf was a testament to her belief in my potential and her dedication to my well-being.

The principal, moved by my mother's plea, granted me permission to enroll in the regular classes. This decision marked a pivotal moment in my life, opening the doors to a world of knowledge and learning that I had longed to be a part of. My mother's faith in me and her unwavering support became the foundation upon which I built my aspirations.

Adapting to school life presented its own set of challenges. Navigating the physical environment was just one aspect; integrating into a community of peers who had little understanding of my journey required patience and resilience. Yet, with each passing day, I found strength in the lessons learned both within and beyond the classroom walls. My teachers and classmates gradually became allies in my quest for knowledge, offering support and encouragement along the way.

Every day, as I navigated my way through the early years of schooling, my mother was there—just outside the classroom, ready to lend a hand whenever I needed. My mother's sacrifices and her dedication to my well-being underscored every step I took, teaching me the true meaning of selflessness and love.

Then there was Sabina, my neighbor and soon-to-be my guiding star. Her family moved in behind our house, and despite our different religious backgrounds—her being Christian and me Hindu—it mattered little. In her, I found a kindred spirit, a friend who looked beyond the physical and saw me for who I truly was. Sabina became more than just a friend; she was my guide, my ally, and a source of endless joy. Together, we explored the world around us, our adventures limited only by our imagination.

Our friendship broke down the barriers that often divide us. With Sabina, I ventured into places I never thought possible. She introduced me to her church, and together, we immersed ourselves in the festivities of Christmas, practicing dance routines to perform in front of the church, our movements in harmony with the music. Dancing became our shared language, a way to express our joy, our hopes, and our dreams. It was through dance that I found a sense of freedom, a way to transcend the limitations that had so often defined me.

As the years went by, Sabina's presence became my strength. She stood by me, not just as a friend but as a protector, assuring my mother that she had nothing to worry about as long as we were together. Our bond deepened, rooted in mutual respect and an unspoken understanding that transcended words.

The challenges of school were many, but they were challenges I was ready to face head-on. The anticipation of final exams, a culmination of our efforts, loomed large. The reward for excellence was not just a trophy but recognition—a chance to prove oneself. When the results were announced, I found myself at the top of the school, a moment of validation that was as much a victory for me as it was for those who believed in me.

Receiving the trophy, the medal, and the prize money in front of the entire school was a surreal experience. I saw pride in my mother's eyes, tears that spoke volumes of the journey we had embarked upon together. My father's pride, my sister's joy, and the sheer surprise in the eyes of those around me served as a reminder of the stereotypes and barriers we had shattered together.

The principal, once doubtful of my abilities, now stood as a witness to my achievement. The look of embarrassment on his face was not lost on me, but it was a moment of gentle vindication rather than triumph. I had proven, not just to him but to everyone, that physical disability did not equate to a lack of capability or intelligence. I was more than my physical limitations; I was a testament to the strength of the human spirit.

The community's reaction was a mix of shock and admiration. Rumors of my success spread like wildfire, challenging long-held perceptions about disability and competence. I had become a living example that one's physical condition does not define one's intellectual or emotional capacity. This realization, spreading through the camp, began to alter the way people saw not just me but perhaps others with disabilities as well.

This journey of mine, marked by challenges, was also filled with moments of profound joy and triumph. From the early struggles of adapting to school life to finding solace and strength in friendships and finally achieving academic success, each step was a testament to the power of perseverance, support, and belief in oneself.

Each day, the journey to school was a testament to resilience and hope, a routine Sabina and I embraced with unwavering purpose. Clasping hands tightly, we traversed the 35-minute walk across the refugee camp, a path devoid of the luxury of transportation but rich in lessons about human behavior and its challenges. This daily trek was more than a physical journey; it was an exploration of the complexities of life and the perseverance it demanded.

One such challenge was the unwelcome attention from other students along the road. Their actions, throwing rocks and mocking my walk and speech, were a harsh reminder of the cruelty that can reside in the hearts of others. Sabina, ever the protector, stood up for me, her spirit unbroken by their taunts. Yet, despite her valiant efforts, the hurtful words and actions found their mark, leaving a wound deeper than the physical.

The culmination of these experiences led to a moment of profound vulnerability. Finding solace in the small temple within my home, I faced the deity that watched over us, a silent witness to the trials of its devotees. Surrounded by pictures of my god, each image a testament to divine grace, I gazed into those serene faces, my heart swelling with a mix of reverence and sorrow. In front of the embodiment of divine presence, I allowed my heart to break open, my tears flowing freely, a river of questioning and despair. As each tear fell, I whispered, "Why did you make me like this? Why can't I be like others?" My voice cracked under the weight of my plea, seeking understanding, yearning for a sign that there was a reason behind the pain, behind the differences that set me apart. The silent images seemed to absorb my sorrow, their steadfast gaze offering a quiet solace in the storm of my emotions.

Upon witnessing this raw display of anguish, my mother found herself overtaken by her own emotions. Stepping outside, she allowed herself a moment of vulnerability, a brief interlude where she, too, questioned the fairness of life's trials. Yet, it was her strength, her unwavering support, that shone through when she returned to my side. Wiping away her tears, she shared words that would become a beacon of hope in my darkest times. "You have a big purpose. That is why God made you special. You are here to change the world."

These words, spoken with the conviction only a mother's love can muster, planted a seed of hope within me. They reminded me that amidst the trials and tribulations, there is a purpose to our existence, a unique path each of us must walk. My mother's faith in me, her belief in my potential to make a difference, became the armor I wore against the slings and arrows of misfortune.

In response to the challenges faced on our daily journey, my father made a decision that would forever alter our routine. The purchase of a motorcycle became a symbol of protection, a means to shield me from the cruelty of the world. It was a gesture that spoke volumes of his love and the lengths to which he would go to ensure my safety and well-being.

Sabina, ever-present, became more than just a friend; she was an extension of our family. Together, we navigated the roads on the motorcycle, a triumphant ride that marked the beginning of a new chapter. It was a declaration that we would not be defined by the actions of others, and that our spirits would remain unbroken.

This journey, marked by trials, was also a testament to the strength found in the love and support of those who stood by me. It taught me that vulnerability is not a weakness but a doorway to strength, and that in our darkest moments, we find the light of hope and the promise of a purpose greater than ourselves. My mother's words, a beacon of hope in the tumultuous sea of life, reminded me that each of us is here for a reason, a unique contribution to the tapestry of existence. And in this realization, I found the courage to face each day with a renewed sense of purpose and determination.

Chapter 5: The Power of Resilience

Every new morning at school brought with it a murmur of surprise that rustled through the classrooms like a soft wind through tall grass. The whispers were never malicious, just tinged with genuine wonder. "How did she do it?" they would ask. "How does she keep being the topper?" I heard their questions, saw their puzzled looks, and felt the weight of their curiosity. But within me, there was no room for doubt, only the space for resolve and the quiet thrill of proving what I knew I could do.

I was a child with a disability, an undeniable part of me, but a part that did not define my entirety. From the tender age of my second-grade year, each academic milestone wasn't just passed; it was conquered. With every grade, my name climbed higher on that esteemed list of achievers until it consistently hovered at the top.

The surprise that marked my early victories gradually turned into a form of respect, a subtle acknowledgment that perhaps there was more to me than met the eye. This respect was sweet, but the self-respect I earned truly colored my days with joy. Each recognition, each trophy, was not just a testament to my intellect but a trophy for my resilience.

When fourth grade dawned, it brought change as profound as the shift from night to day. My school got old, and with that move came a new school. This transition could have been a storm, unsettling the foundations I had built, but I chose to see it as a liberation. It was a chance to prove myself anew, carve my name into fresh halls, and make known the force of my determination in a place where no one knew my story.

At this new school, there were no whispers of surprise, no shadows of past expectations. Here, I was simply another student, a blank slate amidst a sea of possibilities. And it was here that I truly stretched my wings. The anonymity was a challenge, and the lack of expectations was a new kind of freedom. I embraced both with an open heart.

In the heart of my school years, nestled deep within the echoes of academic triumphs, lay a starkly contrasting experience—an experience that would imprint upon me lessons far sterner than those found in textbooks. I had reached the fourth grade, a pinnacle year, where the air buzzed with the electricity of impending adulthood and the finality of school days. But amidst this buzz, a shadow lingered, cast not by the complexities of adolescence but by a figure of authority—a teacher.

In our school, discipline was wielded like a blunt instrument. Those who stumbled in their academic duties and forgot their homework or assignments were often met with a physical reprimand. This form of discipline was a carryover from an older, harsher educational ethos that I had hoped to have escaped.

My parents, aware of my past and protective of my spirit, had made a pact with the principals of my previous schools—a clear, firm agreement: no hand was to be raised against me, not as a means of discipline, not for any reason. This understanding was rooted not just in parental love but in a deep respect for my dignity and my rights as a student and as a person.

As I transitioned into this new school, this agreement was whispered into the ear of the new principal with the same fervor, the same insistence. Yet, somehow, this crucial message faltered along its way to the ears that needed it most.

It was on a day like any other, under the fluorescent glow of classroom lights, that the oversight came to a head. My math and science teacher—a man whose authority was as formidable in sports as it was in academic subjects—called my name. His voice, a harbinger of dread, sliced through the murmurs of my classmates. I had forgotten my homework, an honest lapse, but a lapse nonetheless.

As he moved toward me, the moment stretched, taut as a string. The classroom air felt thick, charged with an impending decision that would violate the sanctuary my parents had so carefully built around me. My heart pounded, not with the fear of forgotten homework but with the shock of potential betrayal.

But the blow never came. Instead, his voice, gruff with disappointment yet free of malice, broke the tension. "Remember your assignments," he admonished, his words a stark reminder rather than a physical reprimand. The relief that flooded me was palpable, not just for the absence of a strike but for the preservation of my trust in this new environment.

The incident sparked a flurry of meetings and conversations drenched in the importance of communication and understanding. My parents, staunch advocates for my education and well-being, reinforced their stance against physical discipline, bridging any gaps in communication that had initially failed us.

While shadowed by the threat of misunderstanding, this episode was illuminated by the lessons it bore. I learned about the power of voice—both in its potential to intimidate and to advocate. I learned about the resilience of agreements and how they must be safeguarded and communicated again and again to protect and to serve. And importantly, I learned about the significance of standing firm in one's values, even—or especially—when they are tested.

The strictness of the school was not just a policy but a palpable, ever-present force, felt most acutely when discipline was meted out with a harshness that left little room for empathy or understanding.

On that fateful day, my name echoed across the room, pulled from the list of those who had failed to complete their homework. The sound of my name, spoken with a stern disappointment, was a prelude to what I knew would follow. It wasn't just me; there were others, too, my peers, who braced for the physical admonition we had come to expect for our lapses. The punishment was arbitrary—a hit on the head or the butt—a demeaning act intended to enforce discipline through fear.

He held a small ruler, a tool that seemed so benign in the hands of others yet so foreboding in his. The moment my head felt the sharp snap of the ruler, a stinging pain radiated through me, not just physically but deep into the crevices of my spirit. Tears welled up, unbidden, streaming down my face as the sting gave way to a profound sense of vulnerability and humiliation.

I remained in my special chair, the one designed to offer the extra space I needed, but now it felt more like a small island in a sea of scrutiny and shame. I couldn't move, couldn't stop the tears that were a silent testament to my pain. My friend Sabina, witnessing my distress, rushed to inform my father, who was waiting outside, ready to whisk me away from this place of learning turned battleground.

The confrontation that ensued was a storm of emotion. My father, a man who had never raised his voice or hand to me, who treated me with the gentlest of touches, was now a visage of anguish and anger. In front of the principal, his words broke through his tears, questioning how a place dedicated to nurturing young minds could justify such brutality. His voice cracked under the weight of his love for me, his despair at the violation of the trust he had placed in the school.

My father's love was a fierce protector, a shield against the injustices of the world. As we left the school that day, his protective arm around my shoulders, he shared wisdom that was both a balm and a lesson. He spoke of the harsh realities of the world, the existence of cruelty, and the inevitability of encountering it. But more importantly, he spoke of resilience, of facing such adversities with strength, even when he wouldn't be there to shield me.

The next day, the change in the air was palpable. The teacher, now a figure of subdued shame, could not meet my eyes. His demeanor had shifted, the arrogance subdued by the sharp rebuke of a grieving father and the silent judgment of his peers. It seemed that the principal's stern admonition had echoed deeper than expected, reminding him of the dignity every student deserved, regardless of the mistakes they made.

From that day on, I carried with me not just the memory of the pain but the powerful lesson of standing up against injustice. My father's tears had been for both of us—mourning a moment of pain but fiercely defending the principle of respect and dignity. More profound than any found in textbooks, this lesson was about the power of a voice raised not in anger but in defense of what is right. It was a lesson about the strength within me, taught through the love and courage of a father who believed in justice and the importance of safeguarding the vulnerable. Despite our middle-class status and living in a refugee camp, my dad always made sure to fulfill every one of my wishes. We were the only family there with access to nice food and clothes, all thanks to his tireless efforts. My parents never let us feel deprived in any way. Additionally, my aunt—my dad's third sister—who lives outside the camp, would send us bags of rice from her large farm where she grows rice and vegetables. She truly is the best aunt, contributing significantly to our well-being with her generosity.

Chapter 6: A New Beginning in America

In the labyrinth of our lives, the darkest corridors were often not those imposed by external misfortunes but carved out by the hands of those we once believed were our guardians. Paradoxically, the villain in our story was my father's cousin—a person who should have been among our protectors. This revision is crucial, as it corrects a painful misrepresentation. The memories remain fraught with confusion and sorrow, but it is important to set the record straight.

Once a figure of strength and assurance in our lives, my father continued to be our steadfast supporter, even as his cousin cast a long shadow over our path to safety and stability. In our bid to leave the refugee camp and start anew in the United States, we faced not only the bureaucratic labyrinth but unexpected sabotage from within our own extended family.

My father's cousin endeavored to undermine our entire resettlement process for reasons known only to him. He contacted the agency responsible for our relocation, spinning a web of deceit. He falsely claimed that we did not belong in the refugee camp and that our roots and our reasons for seeking asylum were fabrications.

The irony of his actions was cruel—especially since, like my father, he was born in Bhutan, the very soil from which we had been uprooted. Yet, he declared otherwise, attempting to distort our legitimate claim to asylum. My father's cousin's motivations seemed murky, laced with the dark undertones of blackmail for money—a concept so foreign and repulsive to our plight that it left us reeling in disbelief.

Why would he do this? This question haunted our days and nights as we grappled with the practical implications of his betrayal. Swayed by his assertions, the agency began to doubt our integrity, questioning the authenticity of our documents and our testimonies. This mistrust stalled our resettlement process, trapping us in a limbo that seemed designed to break our spirits.

Amidst this turmoil, a personal tragedy struck with a ferocity that overwhelmed all else. My mother, already burdened by the uncertainty of our future, received the devastating news that her own mother, my grandmother, had passed away. The news arrived too late, the finality of death rendering our anticipated reunion impossible.

The impact on my mother was profound. The woman who had held us together, who had shielded us with her optimism and relentless hope, crumbled under the weight of her grief. I watched helplessly as she was consumed by her loss, her cries a heart-wrenching soundtrack to our already grim situation.

This period of our lives, marked by the incomprehensible actions of my father's cousin and the grievous loss of my grandmother, was a testament to the complexities of human motives and the fragile nature of familial bonds. It was a chapter where the promise of a new beginning was tainted by the actions of one of our own, where the sanctuary we sought was jeopardized not by external forces but by an internal betrayal.

As we navigated through these darkest times, the lessons were harsh but invaluable. We learned about resilience in the face of profound betrayal, about the strength required to hold onto hope when it is most elusive, and about the painful realization that sometimes those who should protect us can become the very obstacles we need to overcome.

The magic of new beginnings is often shadowed by the trials that forge them, and our journey was no exception. Amidst the turmoil and the betrayals, a flicker of hope was kept alive by our ally—my father, who worked within the very company that was to bring us to the United States. His intervention was a beacon that guided us through our darkest times, helping us to reinitiate the stalled immigration process that my father's cousin had so desperately tried to sabotage.

As the gears of bureaucracy finally turned in our favor, we completed all the necessary requirements, and our move was approved. The reality of leaving our past behind began to set in, marked poignantly by the departure date: May 20. It was a day of painful goodbyes as my entire family from India gathered to see us off. Tears were shed, promises to keep in touch were made, and the heavy weight of farewell hung over us all. It was a heart-wrenching reminder that while we were pursuing a dream, it meant leaving a part of our lives behind forever.

It was 23rd May 2016, a pivotal moment in my young life as my family and I stepped onto American soil, embarking on a journey filled with unknowns. The journey itself was a flurry of new experiences and daunting challenges. My first time on an airplane was marked by a mix of excitement and profound fear. The vast, open skies were as intimidating as they were awe-inspiring. Landing in America, the land that promised refuge and opportunity, was surreal. Yet, the airport was a labyrinth, and our family, carrying the burden of hope and apprehension, felt starkly out of place.

Compounding our challenges was my condition—cerebral palsy. At a layover in New York on our way to Pennsylvania, misunderstanding and prejudice briefly barred our way. Authorities were misinformed about my health and hesitated to allow me to continue traveling. It was a stark introduction to the obstacles we would face, even in a land that prided itself on diversity and opportunity. My mother, armed with her limited English, advocated fiercely for me, explaining that cerebral palsy was not a sickness that should prevent me from flying. Her strength in that moment was a profound testament to the protective love of a parent.

Finally arriving in Pittsburgh, we were enveloped by the familiar yet distant faces of relatives. My cousins, aunt, and uncle, along with my grandfather, welcomed us. The reunion was bittersweet—joyous yet marred by the absence of my grandmother, whose passing had been a sharp pain in our hearts. Despite the warmth of their welcome, exhaustion and the disorientation of time changes left me in a daze, struggling to take it all in.

I was just twelve, with the world seemingly vast and intimidating, especially as I faced the reality of entering a new school where I could not speak the language. The prospect of starting sixth grade at Harrison Middle School stirred a tumultuous mix of fear and excitement within me.

From the very first day, amid the maze of unfamiliar faces and indecipherable words, one person stood out—Mrs. Tkach.

Although the English words she spoke were just strange sounds to my ears, her smiles were a universal language, painting feelings of warmth and safety that I understood perfectly. Her patience was a gentle ocean, calming the storm of anxieties that threatened to overwhelm me. It didn't take long for me to realize that she was more than just a support person; she was a guardian in this new chapter of my life.

Mrs. Tkach's presence brought a sense of comfort that reminded me of home, of my mother's nurturing. Even though we were separated before the school year ended due to a change in her schedule, our bond was indelible. Her assurance that we would reunite was a beacon of hope. More importantly, she left me with words that would anchor me throughout my schooling years: "God never gives us more than he knows we can handle." She believed in my strength and foresaw greatness in my future, a belief I gradually embraced.

Middle school was a transformative period. With each passing day, I not only improved my English but also wove myself into the fabric of the school community. I made friends who were both curious and accepting, teachers who were encouragers and guides, and together, they helped me navigate the complexities of this new world.

The journey to a new land is often painted with the hues of hope and new beginnings. But for some, like my family and me, a tragic undertone shadowed this journey, a stark contrast to the dreams we carried in our hearts. The United States beckoned with the promise of refuge, which seemed within reach, only obscured by unexpected betrayal.

Our new home, while a sanctuary in theory, struck my senses harshly at first—everything unfamiliar and foreign, including the very air I breathed, which seemed starkly different from what I had known. Adjusting to these new surroundings was not just a matter of unpacking bags but of unpacking old fears and insecurities, making room for new hopes and dreams.

Here I am now, in this new chapter, where the narrative of my life continues to unfold. The journey from a refugee camp to the heart of Pittsburgh is not just a physical transition but a transformation of every facet of my existence. It's a continual process of finding my place in this vast, sprawling tapestry of cultures and experiences that is America. With each passing day, I learn a little more about this new world and, in turn, about myself. Each challenge faced, each barrier overcome, teaches me that while the path to fulfillment is seldom easy, it is always worth the journey.

Chapter 7: Finding My Voice

Growing up, English was not my first language, which posed a significant barrier when I began school in the United States. I vividly remember stepping into my sixth-grade classroom, filled with apprehension and a profound sense of isolation. The language spoken around me was one I could barely comprehend, let alone speak. This linguistic barrier transformed what should have been an exciting learning environment into an overwhelming challenge.

In sixth grade, I found myself lost in translations. As my classmates engaged actively with the lessons, I struggled to grasp even the basic instructions. The teacher's words seemed to float around me, a jumble of sounds I couldn't decipher into meaningful sentences. This communication gap affected my academic performance severely. While other students handed in completed assignments and participated in discussions, I grappled with understanding the questions. My grades reflected this immense challenge, and my GPA suffered as a result. I felt discouraged, watching my peers excel while I lagged behind, trying to decode a foreign language.

However, as I transitioned into seventh grade, the persistent cloud of confusion began to lift gradually. I started to decipher what my teachers and classmates were saying. Words and phrases that once sounded alien began to make sense. This breakthrough was more than just academic; it was emotional. Understanding English allowed me to connect with others and express my thoughts and needs.

With determination, I immersed myself in learning; I watched English movies, read books, and practiced speaking as much as possible. My efforts began to pay off in remarkable ways. Not only did my comprehension improve, but I also became more confident in using English to communicate. My grades started to reflect my increased understanding and newfound confidence. By the end of the year, my GPA had risen significantly, and I earned a high honor award, a recognition that seemed impossible just a year before.

As I transitioned from middle school to high school, the trepidation of stepping into a more challenging educational environment was palpable. Having overcome my initial language barriers, I was excited but nervous about the new opportunities and challenges that high school would bring. This next chapter of my educational journey brought advanced coursework and a deeper discovery of my interests and talents, particularly in literature and writing.

In eighth grade, amidst improving my English and acclimating to a new academic culture, I discovered a profound love for reading and writing. Books became my refuge; they were not just a tool for language learning but gateways to different worlds and experiences. I found solace and excitement in poetry and essays, which allowed me to express myself in ways I had never imagined possible. This newfound passion was not just a hobby but a lifeline that connected me to the core of my creative self.

Entering ninth grade, my initial nervousness quickly transformed into enthusiasm as I began to explore various literary forms more deeply. The supportive environment and the encouragement of my teachers fueled my passion, allowing me to excel in my literature and writing classes. This period was a significant affirmation of my abilities and my decision to embrace English not just as a second language but as a medium for artistic expression.

However, just as I was finding my stride, the global pandemic hit. The sudden shift to online learning during my tenth grade was a jarring disruption. The isolation and the impersonal nature of digital classrooms posed a new set of challenges. The interactive and engaging learning environment I had grown to love was replaced by screens and virtual spaces. Despite these obstacles, my determination did not waver. I adapted to the new learning modalities and managed to achieve high grades, a testament to the resilience and adaptability I had developed over the years.

By eleventh grade, the return to in-person learning brought a familiar face back into my life— Mrs Tkach, a support person who had been instrumental in my earlier academic journey. Having her support again felt like reuniting with a part of my extended family. Her guidance was crucial as I navigated the complexities of higher-level education and prepared for the future. Her presence in the classroom rekindled my academic enthusiasm and reinforced my commitment to my studies and my creative pursuits.

As my high school years unfolded, each day brought new experiences that shaped my personal and academic growth. Among the pivotal moments of my journey, two standout experiences profoundly impacted me: the mentorship of Mrs. Tkach, whom I affectionately called my "school mom," and a life-changing opportunity through the Bender Leadership Academy.

Mrs. Tkach was more than just a support person at school; she became a mentor and a part of my family. As described in the sixth chapter of my book, her role extended beyond traditional school responsibilities. Whether I needed help with schoolwork, advice on personal matters, or simply someone to talk to, Mrs. Tkach was there. Her unwavering kindness and emotional support were beacons of stability, making her my "school mom." Her encouragement was a crucial factor in my resilience and success, lightening the load of each challenging day.

In eleventh grade, another teacher recognized my potential and introduced me to the Bender Leadership Academy. This program was designed to empower individuals with disabilities, teaching them vital skills needed for employment and independence. The academy also focused on leadership training, encouraging participants to take active roles in their communities.

As part of my involvement with the academy, I was tasked with writing and delivering a speech. The topic was deeply personal—I spoke about my experiences with bullying and how I overcame them. The act of sharing my story in front of 300 people was both daunting and cathartic. As I stood there, words flowing with a mixture of pain and triumph, I found myself overwhelmed with emotion. Tears streamed down my face, not just from the memories of past hardships but from a profound sense of accomplishment and the heartfelt reactions from the audience.

Speaking in front of 300 people, I discussed my personal challenges and achievements and the profound impact my siblings had on my life. The audience's response was overwhelmingly emotional; many were moved to tears, reflecting the power and relatability of my experiences. That speech was a turning point for me. It highlighted the importance of vulnerability and the strength it takes to share one's struggles openly. It also demonstrated the impact of personal growth and how overcoming challenges can inspire others. My journey through bullying to a place of leadership and advocacy had a powerful resonance, giving voice to those who felt silenced.

Navigating the complexities of school and personal growth took on even more meaning during my formative years with the arrival of new family members. The births of my sister and brother not only brought joy and happiness but also shaped my identity and responsibilities within my family.

In seventh grade, a significant milestone marked my journey—not just in school but in my personal life—my sister Saina was born. Her arrival during a pivotal time in my academic and personal development brought a new sense of joy and purpose. As I struggled and eventually succeeded in overcoming language barriers, Saina's presence added a layer of motivation. She became a source of inspiration, reminding me of the importance of perseverance and the joy of achieving goals not just for myself but for the sake of my family.

By the time I reached eleventh grade, another profound event occurred—my brother Ishaan was born. Ishaan's arrival during another crucial phase of my life, as I was preparing to leave high school and enter adulthood, deepened my sense of responsibility. I often describe Ishaan not merely as a brother but in many ways as a son, a soulmate, and my best friend, despite his young age. At two years old, Ishaan already showed a unique understanding and a special bond with me. He became not just a sibling but a confidant and a source of unconditional love and joy.

Senior year of high school often marks the pinnacle of one's educational journey—a year filled with last times, significant achievements, and a final farewell to the formative years before stepping into the wider world. For me, senior year was not just about academic achievements and future plans; it was profoundly shaped by friendships and memorable experiences that I will cherish forever.

During my senior year at Baldwin High School, I was fortunate to solidify friendships that began to bloom in earlier years. While I met Sano back in seventh grade, our friendship didn't deepen until much later. During our senior year, we truly connected alongside another classmate, Lokey, whom I met during a lively moment at the senior recreational dance. Lokey was effortlessly dancing, and that joyous atmosphere helped spark what would become a deep and lasting bond among us. We three became inseparable, supporting each other through the ups and downs of that pivotal year. These friendships provided a source of comfort, laughter, and strength, enriching my senior year exponentially.

Senior year was filled with both fun and academic pursuits. The joy of being with my true friends made every school day enjoyable. We shared classes, lunches, and countless memories, each moment bringing us closer. The camaraderie and support from Sano and Lokey became my favorite person, part of my family, and best friend!

As the year drew to a close, graduation day was a bittersweet culmination of all our high school experiences. It was a moment of immense pride and joy, tinged with the sadness of saying goodbye to a significant chapter of our lives. Walking down the aisle, I was overwhelmed with a mix of emotions. Mrs Tkach, my mentor and "school mom," was there to support me, just as she had been throughout my high school journey. Her presence was a comforting reminder of how far I had come—from a struggling newcomer in sixth grade to a confident graduate ready to take on the world.

Chapter 8: Dreams and Determination

From the moment of my siblings' births, my connection with my younger brother and sister has been nothing short of miraculous. As the elder sibling, my journey with them has been filled with profound affection and mutual understanding, which has significantly shaped who I am today. At the tender age of two, my brother exudes a level of empathy and connection that is truly heartwarming. He demonstrates his love in the simplest yet most impactful ways, such as sharing his food with me, a gesture that speaks volumes about his character. It's this unconditional love that has taught me the essence of family and compassion.

My sister, who is soon to turn seven, brings another dimension of joy into my life. As she grows, her personality blossoms, revealing traits of both sensitivity and exuberance. Our bond is a tapestry of shared secrets, laughter, and support, which grows richer with each passing day. Observing her navigate through her formative years with curiosity and zeal is a continuous source of inspiration.

As much as I cherish these moments of sibling camaraderie and the purity of childhood innocence, I am also navigating my path toward personal and professional growth. Currently, I am enrolled in a community college, a strategic choice that serves as a stepping stone toward a broader academic and career trajectory. My plan is to complete two years here before transferring to the University of Pittsburgh to major in political science.

This career path was not chosen on a whim. It is deeply personal and rooted in my own life experiences. As someone who has navigated the complexities of living with a disability, I am acutely aware of the challenges and obstacles that can arise. My academic and career goals are driven by a desire to advocate for and support individuals with disabilities. I aim to ensure that others do not have to endure the hardships I face and to work toward a society where inclusivity is not just an ideal but a reality.

The field of political science fascinates me because it offers the tools and knowledge necessary to effect change. By understanding the intricacies of government systems and policies and how they impact society, I believe I can make a significant impact. My ambition is to specialize in policymaking that prioritizes the needs and rights of disabled individuals, advocating for reforms that are long overdue.

Balancing my college education with family life presents its challenges, but it is a fulfilling endeavor. Every lesson learned and every hurdle overcome in college is a step closer to my goal of becoming a champion for those in need. Meanwhile, the unwavering support from my family fuels my resolve to succeed. They are not just my motivation but also my sanctuary, providing love and encouragement through every phase of my journey.

As I sit down to share this part of my journey, I reflect on the profound impact that my work at Bender Consulting Service is having, not just on my life but on the lives of many others. It's an incredible feeling to be at the forefront of a movement that champions employment opportunities for people with disabilities, a cause that's not only noble but essential.

I joined Bender Consulting a few months ago, driven by a desire to make a meaningful difference. This internship has turned out to be more than just a step in my career—it has been a leap into a world where I can be the change I wish to see. At Bender, we're not just advocates; we're catalysts for change. The atmosphere here is charged with positivity and purpose, thanks to the leadership and vision of Joy, our CEO.

Joyce Bender is not just a boss. She's a beacon of inspiration and a testament to what visionary leadership should look like. Under her guidance, Bender Consulting doesn't just operate as a business; it thrives as a community that uplifts each individual. Working alongside her and Jill, my supervisor, whose expertise and encouragement have been pivotal, I've learned not only the intricacies of our work but also the impact of empathy and support in a professional setting.

Every day at Bender is a new opportunity to learn and grow. We collaborate closely, brainstorming and executing strategies that aim to bridge the gap between capable, talented individuals with disabilities and industries that benefit from their skills. This isn't just about employment; it's about creating inclusive environments where everyone has the chance to succeed and contribute meaningfully.

Our approach is straightforward yet effective. We identify potential employment opportunities, tailor our training programs to meet the specific needs of our clients and support them through every step of their employment journey. This hands-on method ensures that we're not only helping individuals find jobs but also helping them thrive in their roles, fostering a sense of accomplishment and independence.

What makes this experience even more rewarding is the familial atmosphere at Bender. Despite being one of six family members at home, where love and support are a given, finding a similar environment at work was unexpected. Bender has become my second family. Here, everyone is treated with respect and dignity, and every success is celebrated collectively.

As I progress through my internship, my commitment to this cause deepens. Witnessing firsthand the challenges faced by people with disabilities in the job market has fortified my resolve to advocate for equity and accessibility. The satisfaction of seeing our clients succeed, of knowing that we played a part in their journey, is indescribable.

I am grateful for this opportunity at Bender Consulting Service. It has shaped me in ways I never anticipated. As I continue to work and learn here, I am not just hoping to inspire others through my actions but also continuously inspired by the people I meet, the stories I hear, and the lives we touch. This isn't just a job; it's a mission—one that I am proud to be part of.

Reflecting back on my life, my cousin Smrity moved to the USA from New Delhi, India, in December 2022 and started living with us. She is ten years older than me, and we were very close back in India, especially with my older sister, Isha. In our culture, we don't refer to our cousins as "cousins;" we call them "sisters" or "brothers." Thus, she became our eldest sister! I absolutely adore her!

Recently, while Smrity was on a FaceTime call with her friends back in India, she introduced me to her best friend, Shesme. They are like siblings, though they are not related. Shesme and I began talking, and I learned he was going through a tough time. Smrity assured me that Shesme is a good, kind person, and she was happy for us when we started dating on January 16, 2023. Although we have never met in person, our relationship has grown strong over the distance.

Love, for us, isn't just about physical touch—it's about loving someone without seeing them and falling for their words and conversations. We frequently FaceTime and have introduced each other to our families. It's been over a year now, and we are still together, proving that love needs to be patient, strong, and pure. Shesme and I plan to meet in person next year after I complete two years of community college.

If I talk about my mother, I would not be here writing this book if it weren't for her. My mom is more than a God to me; she has always been my guiding light. She dedicated her life to helping people with disabilities as a special education teacher in Nepal, and her passion has deeply inspired me.

Just as my mom inspired me, I want to be a beacon of hope and inspiration for those with disabilities. I will not let her struggles and sacrifices go to waste. I want people to know my name, just as the fortune teller once said they would.

God made me who I am, and I accept myself wholeheartedly. I am incredibly proud of who I have become. I am Rushma Kafley.

Chapter 9: Embracing My Story

As I reflect on my journey, I am filled with a profound sense of pride and accomplishment. Embracing my identity and disability has been a transformative experience, shaping me into the person I am today. Each step along this path has reinforced my strength, resilience, and determination.

My journey began with challenges that seemed insurmountable. Growing up, I often felt different, out of place, and limited by my disability. Society's expectations and the stigma attached to my condition weighed heavily on me. But rather than letting these obstacles define me, I chose to define myself. I realized that my disability was not a barrier but a unique aspect of my identity that I could embrace with pride.

One of the most significant turning points in my journey was when I decided to take control of my narrative. I stopped viewing my disability as a weakness and started seeing it as a source of strength. This shift in perspective was not easy. It required a deep introspection and a conscious effort to challenge the limiting beliefs I had internalized.

My achievements are a testament to this newfound strength. Every milestone I reached, whether it was academic success, professional accomplishments, or personal growth, served as a marker of my resilience. I learned to celebrate these victories, no matter how small, as they represented my triumphs over adversity.

For instance, completing my education was a monumental achievement. The academic environment was often not accommodating, and I had to navigate numerous hurdles to access the resources I needed. But I persevered. I sought out mentors, utilized support systems, and developed strategies to excel despite the challenges. Graduating with honors was not just a personal victory; it was a symbol of my determination and hard work.

Embracing my identity also meant advocating for others like me. I became involved in disability rights movements, working to create more inclusive environments. This advocacy work was deeply fulfilling. It allowed me to use my experiences to help others and to contribute to a broader societal change. Through public speaking, writing, and activism, I shared my story and encouraged others to see disability through a different lens.

I am proud of how far I have come. My journey is about overcoming obstacles and embracing who I am with pride and confidence. My disability is a part of me, but it does not define me. Instead, it has shaped me into a resilient, empathetic, and determined person.

To my readers, I offer this heartfelt message: look beyond your limitations. Every individual has unique challenges, but these do not have to dictate your life's path. Approach life with courage, determination, and a positive outlook. Your limitations can become your strengths if you choose to see them that way.

Life is a journey filled with ups and downs. Embrace each experience as an opportunity to grow and learn. Surround yourself with supportive people who believe in you and your potential. Seek out mentors, build a network, and never be afraid to ask for help. Remember that asking for support is not a sign of weakness but a recognition of your humanity.

Cultivate a positive mindset. Challenges are inevitable, but how you respond to them is within your control. Develop resilience by focusing on your goals and staying committed to them, even when the path is difficult. Celebrate your achievements, no matter how small, and use them as motivation to keep moving forward.

Finally, believe in yourself. Self-belief is the foundation of success. Trust that you have the strength and capability to overcome any obstacle. Your journey may be different from others, but it is uniquely yours. Embrace it with pride and confidence, knowing that each step you take is a testament to your resilience and determination.

As I delve deeper into my reflections, one belief stands out prominently: the power of perseverance. Throughout my journey, perseverance has been my guiding light, a steadfast force that has carried me through countless challenges. It is this unyielding determination that has enabled me to transform obstacles into opportunities and setbacks into stepping stones toward success.

Perseverance is not just about enduring hardships; it is about continually striving toward your goals, no matter the difficulties you encounter. There were times when the road seemed impossibly long and fraught with barriers. Yet, it was in these moments of adversity that my resolve was tested and strengthened. Each challenge I faced became a testament to my tenacity, a reminder that perseverance is the key to overcoming even the most daunting obstacles.

But perseverance alone is not enough. Equally crucial in my journey has been the unwavering support from my loved ones. Family, friends, mentors, and even kind strangers have played an indispensable role in helping me navigate life's challenges. Their belief in me, their encouragement, and their unwavering support have been the bedrock upon which I built my resilience.

Support from loved ones manifests in various forms. It is the comforting presence of family members who stand by you in your darkest hours, offering words of encouragement and a shoulder to lean on. It is the friends who celebrate your victories, no matter how small, and remind you of your worth when you doubt yourself. It is the mentors who provide guidance and wisdom, helping you to see possibilities where you saw none. It is the community that rallies around you, offering support and resources to help you achieve your goals.

This network of support has been instrumental in my journey. I recall countless instances where the encouragement of a loved one made all the difference. Whether it was a word of advice during a difficult decision, a gesture of kindness when I felt overwhelmed, or simply the silent assurance of their presence, these moments of support have been pivotal.

The core message of my journey, and indeed of this book, is one of resilience and acceptance. Resilience is not just the ability to bounce back from setbacks but the capacity to grow stronger through adversity. It is about embracing challenges as opportunities for growth and recognizing that each obstacle you overcome adds to your strength.

Acceptance, on the other hand, is about acknowledging and embracing your unique identity, including your limitations and imperfections. It is about understanding that these aspects do not diminish your worth but contribute to your uniqueness. Acceptance allows you to move forward with confidence, knowing that you are not defined by your challenges but by how you respond to them.

Empathy, support, and love are transformative forces in navigating life's challenges. Empathy allows us to connect with others on a deep, human level, fostering understanding and compassion. Support from loved ones provides the strength and encouragement needed to face adversity with courage. Love, in all its forms, is the most powerful force of all, inspiring us to persevere and thrive.

I celebrate these transformative powers. They have not only helped me overcome my own challenges but have also inspired me to help others do the same. By sharing my story, I hope to offer a beacon of hope and encouragement to those who may be facing their own struggles.

I urge you to embrace perseverance, seek and cherish the support of your loved ones, and approach life with courage. Remember that you are not alone on this journey. The strength of your perseverance, coupled with the support and love from those around you, can help you overcome any obstacle. Celebrate your victories, learn from your setbacks, and always move forward with resilience and acceptance.

Reflecting on my experiences, I've come to understand that letting problems talk behind your back doesn't change who you are. It's a lesson that has profoundly shaped my outlook on life. Problems and challenges will always be there, but they don't define us. Instead, they are opportunities to learn and grow. I've learned that God gave us two ears so that we can let negative things in one ear and out the other, refusing to let them linger and affect our spirit.

Kindness has been a cornerstone of my life. I taught myself that being kind doesn't detract from anything; instead, it enriches lives—both mine and others. When you show kindness to people, the world responds in kind. It's like a circle; kindness comes back to you, often when you least expect it. This reciprocity of kindness has been a powerful revelation for me, reinforcing my belief in the goodness of people and the impact we can have on each other's lives.

Every success story has its struggles. Without struggle, there is no hope for success. This truth has been evident throughout my journey. Struggles are not setbacks; they are the crucibles in which our strengths are forged. They test our resolve and shape our character, preparing us for the successes that lie ahead. I've learned to embrace struggles as part of the journey, knowing that they bring hope and pave the way for future achievements.

God has always been a guiding force in my life. Choosing the right path, even when it's difficult, has brought me peace and guidance. I believe that God is always there for us, providing support and direction if we choose to follow the path of righteousness and integrity.

Growing up, I realized that while the world can be cruel, there are also many kind-hearted people. This duality taught me the importance of surrounding myself with positive influences and being one myself. I learned to respect my elders and show love to the younger generation. Respect and love are fundamental values that create a supportive and nurturing environment for everyone.

Looking ahead, my vision for the future is one where I continue to break barriers and advocate for inclusivity and understanding. I aim to be a voice for those who feel marginalized and overlooked, working toward a society where everyone is valued and respected, regardless of their abilities or background. My journey is far from over, and I am committed to making a difference, one step at a time.

I envision a world where empathy and compassion are the norms, where people look out for each other and work together to overcome challenges. By sharing my story and experiences, I hope to inspire others to embrace their own journeys with optimism and resilience. We all have the power to make a positive impact in the lives of others, and I encourage everyone to take that responsibility to heart.

To my readers, I want to say this: embrace your journey, no matter how difficult it may seem. Every struggle is an opportunity to grow stronger and wiser. Approach life with a positive outlook, knowing that you have the power to make a difference. Show kindness to those around you, respect your elders, and love the younger generation. These simple acts can transform lives and create a ripple effect of positivity and goodwill.

Remember that success is often preceded by struggle. Don't be discouraged by setbacks; instead, use them as stepping stones to achieve your goals. Keep your faith strong, trust in God's plan, and choose the right path, even when it's the harder one. Your journey is unique and valuable, and your experiences can inspire others.

www.ingramcontent.com/pod-product-compliance
Lightning Source LLC
Chambersburg PA
CBHW040829120726

48005CB00012B/1551